WEB DESIGN

Contents

INTRODUCTION TO HTML

Before starting let me tell you that you should not skip any section because this is a very short book and everything is given very directly.

1.1 Guidelines for HTML

Html allows web designers to create websites. A designer must follow this rules-

a) Structure and presentation must be separated so that designer and developer can work independently. This can be done by creating style sheets.

b) Your website should be universally accessible.

1.2 META element

Metadata refers to information about the data within the document. It can be author, content, keywords, information or any details. In html *meta* element is declared within head element.

```
<HTML>
<HEAD>
<TITLE>HTML</TITLE>
<META name="AUTHOR" content="ABHISHEK"/>
<META name="KEYWORDS" content="WEB DESIGNING"/>
</HEAD>
<BODY>
LEARN TO MAKE A WEBSITE
```

```
</BODY>
</HTML>
```

1.3 TEXT PROPERTIES

We can apply many properties to text. Such as bold, italic, underline and we can change type of font also.

```
<html>

<b>learn to make a website</b>

<i> learn to make a website</i>

<u> learn to make a website</u>

<font face=Algerian>learn to make a website</font>

</html>
```

Output-learn to make a website

Learn to make website

<u>Learn to make website</u>

LEARN TO MAKE WEBSITE

1.4 Basic properties of html

Some basic properties like to leave a line, to draw a line, to move a text or image.

```
<html>
learn to make a website<br>
<i> learn to make a website<br>
<hr>
</html>
```

-to move image or text

```
<html>
<marquee>learn to make a website</marquee>
</html>
```

1.5 Image properties

To bring a image to your page use the code

```
<html>
```

```
<img src="address of your image"
height=70px width=100px;/>
```

```
</html>
```

If your image not coming then the address of your image is wrong then

go to the image and open with it your browser and copy the address of image above it.

1.6 Ordered lists

```
<html>
```

```
<body>
```

```
<h>colors</h>
```

```
<UL>
```

```
<LI>vibgyor</LI>
```

```
<UL style="list-style-type:square">
```

```
<LI>violet</LI>
```

```
<LI>indigo</LI>
```

```
<LI>blue</LI>>
```

```
<LI>GREEN<LI>

<LI>YELLOW<LI>

<LI>ORANGE</LI>

</UL>

</UL>

</body>

</html>
```

COLORS

- **VIBGYOR**
  - **VIOLET**
  - **INDIGO**
  - **GREEN**
  - **YELLOW**
  - **ORANGE**

1.7 Background properties

Background properties consists of background color and background image. For background image use

```
<html>

<body background="address of image">

</body>

</html>
```

For background color use

```
<html>

<body bgcolor="red">

</body

</html>
```

TABLE PROPERTIES

Now a days tables are not used in website because we use style instead of table but since in any case you need a table in your webpage, this chapter is going to help you completely.

NAME	TOTAL	PERCENTAGE
A	2132	34
S	1232	23
D	4214	45
F	3424	34
GRAND TOTAL	4	

```
<html>

<body>

<table width="900" height="220"
border="10">

<thead>

 <tr>

   <th width="185" height="30"> NAME</th>

   <th width="304">TOTAL</th>

   <th width="371">PERCENTAGE</th>

 </tr>
```

```html
</thead>
<tr>
  <td>A</td>
  <td>2132</td>
  <td>34</td>
</tr>
<tr>
  <td>S</td>
  <td>1232</td>
  <td>23</td>
</tr>
<tr>
  <td>D</td>
  <td>4214</td>
  <td>45</td>
</tr>
<tr>
```

```html
      <td>F</td>

      <td>3424</td>

      <td>34</td>

    </tr>

    <tr>

      <td>TOTAL STUDENTS</td>

      <td>4</td>

      <td> </td>

    </tr>

  </table>

</body>

</html>
```

In these codes <thead> is used for the head columns of the table.

<tr> code is used to enter in a row.

<td> code is used to enter in a column.

If you are really want to make a website I suggest you to use dreamweaver

Because in this software you don't need to type the whole code of a tale so it will help you to make table as well as it will help you to remember codes also.

There are one more kind of a table.

1		3	4
2			

```
<table width="900" border="10">

  <tr>

    <td>&1</td>

    <td rowspan="2">&3</td>

    <td rowspan="2">&4</td>

  </tr>

  <tr>

    <td>&2</td>

  </tr>

  <tr>
```

```
<td>&5</td>

<td>&6</td>

<td>&7</td>

</tr>

</table>
```

In this table the main component is rowspan which divides the row in two rows.

If you want to divide a column, you can use colspan instead of rowspan.

FORMS AND FRAMES

Forms and frames are the essential part of a wepage. Almost in every website you are going to find a form as well as several frames in it.

First we are going to start with forms-

```
<HTML>

<form>

<label>NAME   : </label><input type="text" /><br /><br />

<label>OCCUPATION:  </label><input type="text" /><br /><br />

<label>ADDRESS:</label><input type="text" /><br /><br />
```

```html
<label>PIN CODE:</label><input type="text" /><br /><br />

<label>GENDER:</label><input type="text" /><br /><br />

<label>PROFFESION:</label><input type="text" /><br /><br />

<input type="button" / value="SUBMIT">

<input type="button" / value="RESET">

</form>

</HTML>
```

OUTPUT

OCCU

PIN

(

PROF

| SUBMIT | RESET |

YOU CAN SEE FROM THIS CODES THAT LEARNING HTML IS VERY EASY.

Now let me explain you how it works;

For starting form we need to declare<form>tag

Input type is used for declare the type of field you need, it can be text, password, address, number. You can see that label is used to give a name to a text field. Label is used to give a name to a text field and value is used to a name to a button.

3.2 FRAMES

FRAMES are used when you want to divide a webpage into several pages. It provides user to simultaneously have multiple views of the webpage. This is done by splitting the browser window into multiple screens. Frames can contain hyperlinks that allow webpage designer to link one frame to another frame. The frame for which a link should be established is known as Source frame and the frame from which a link should be established is known as Target frame.

Lets see a example-

<html>

<frameset cols="30%, 70%>

<frame src="address of the webpage.html">

<frame src="address of other webpage.html">

</frameset>

</html>

In this example the first <frameset cols>is
used when you want to divide a page

Into two or more parts. The first <frame src> tag is used link the first part of webpage which in this case is 30% and second <frame src> tag is used to link another part of webpage. Let us

```
<html>
<frameset cols="30%, 70%>
<frame src="address of the webpage.html">
<frameset rows="50%, 50%>
<frame src="address of other webpage.html">
<frame src="address of other webpage.html">
</frameset>
</html>
```

In this we have divided the second frame into two different frames but in this case we have used <frameset rows> instead of <frameset cols> because we have divided second frame horizontally and <frameset cols> is used when you divide the frame vertically. If you want to divide in another frames, then first create a frame then instead of frame src of this frame create another frameset to divide it in more parts.

INTRODUCTION TO CSS

4.1 **CASCADING STYLE SHEETS**

html had certain limitations such as lack of uniform view of webpage on different browser. In this case of problem css is used. I am not going to tell you that when it was invented or what all versions are there because it is a waste of time and I don't think that you want it.

A style sheet defines styles for parent, child, and descendant elements.

<body>.......................parent

<p>............child

<b>first web page</b>.......descendent

</body>

<p> tag is used for paragraph , whenever you write a paragraph just write a <p>tag in start and end of it.

Lets don't waste time and see a example-

```html
<html>
<head>
<title>first web page</title>
<style type="text/css">
Body
{font family: verdana;
Font-size: 10pt;
}
P,b
{font weight: normal;
}
</style>
</head>
<body>
<p>
<b>this is my page<?b>
</p>
```

```
</body>
</html>
```

Now let us understand how it works,

We have declared style with <style> tag and as we know we need to always end a tag when it is started.

then we have created a class body and in that part we have declared the type of font and size then we have created two other classes p andb in which we have said the font to not change with type of browser.

Then we have written ***this is my first page*** is written in body tag then paragraph tag and then bold tag so all the properties of bold, p, b directly applies to the written text.

I am still suggest you to use dream weaver it will help you completely with the codes.

4.2 IMPORTING STYLE SHEETS

You can create a separate file in notepad or dreamweaver and than you can save it as name.css and then you can import your style sheet to the main page by

```
<html>

<style>

@import "name.css";

</style>

</html>
```

4.3 TEXT PROPERTIES

It helps you to format textual content on the webpage. Some properties are direction, letter-spacing, white-space. This properties are used in class in css only.

```
<style type="text/css">

P

{direction:rt1;

Letter-spcing:1px;
```

```
}
</style>
```

Direction is used to assign the direction to a text and letter pacing is used to provide space between letters.

4.4 MULTIPLE BACKGROUNDS

Background affect the visual appearance of an html page. A webpage can have

multiple background to highlight different sections in it.

```
<html>
<head>
<LINK rel="stylesheet"  type="text/css" href="sac.css">
</head>
<body>
<div class ="ban">
<h2>WEB DEVELOPER</h2>
```

```html
</div>

<div class="se">

<h3>WE DESIGN</h3>

TO MAKE WEBSITE REMEMBER TO BE CREATIVE AND CONCENTRATE.

</div>

<div class="se">

<h3>CSS</h3>

CASCADING STYLE SHEETS HELPS YOU TO DESIGN WEBSITE AND TO MAKE
THEM PROPERLY ARRANGED.

</div>

</body>

<html>
```

CODE-2

```css
Body

{ background:"red.jpg";

Margin: 10px 10px 10px 75px;

}
```

```
.ban

{ background-color:white;

Text-align:center;

}

.se

{background: url('purple.jpg) fixed;

}
```

WEB DEVELOPER

WEBSITE:

TO MAKE WEBSITE REMEMBER TO BE CREATIVE AND CONCENTRATE.

CSS:

CASCADING STYLE SHEETS HELPS YOU TO DESIGN WEBSITE AND TO MAKE THEM PROPERLY ARRANGED.

LETS see what the codes are all about:-

Css codes

We have created two pages in notepad from which one is html and other one is saved with sac.css , let us first understand the css part which says that we have created a body class and we have declared the background image of the page. Then in another class which is

ban we have decided the background color

of that id and said that the text should be

in center. In third class ".se" , we have declared the background image of that

class.Let me tell you one more thing that if we make a class by the name which is

already a function like body class so we don't need to call it its features will automatically will be called when we use<body> tag but classes like "se" and "ban" which is not a predifened function so we need to make a class by ".se" or".ban" .

Html codes

In html call the"sac.css" page by <link rel="stylesheet" type="text/css" href="sac.css"/>tag. Then to call a class which is not predefined like "ban" use

<div class="ban"> and directly all properties of ban class which is in sac.css will be applied to the text between first <div class="ban"> to </ban> and same we have done with se.

4.5 MULTIPLE BORDERS

Designer ca create picture frames by specifying multiple borders using the CSS border properties.

- Html
- Css
- javascript

lets see the codes

```
<html>

<head>

<link rel ="stylesheet" type="text/css" href="project.css"/>
```

```html
</head>
<body>
<hr>
<div class="borderone">
<div class="bordertwo">
<u>
<li>html</li>
<li>css</li>
<li>javascript</li>
</ul>
</div>
</div>
</body>
</html>
```

:-css page

```css
.borderone
{border: 2px solid black;
```

}

.bordertwo

{border: 4px dotted red;

Margin:5px 5px 5px 5px;

Background-color: green;

}

Now let see what this codes are all about:-

Follow the steps:-

→create two pages in notepad one for .html and one for project.css

→call the css page in html by<link rel="stylesheet" type="text/css"

   href="project.css">

→in project.css create two classes for two border and apply the properties

→call both the classes in html by using div element and write one class in

   Another because there is one border in another.

ADVANCED CSS PROPERTIES

CSS allows web designer to position the webpage content anywhere on the webpage.

DIFFERENCE BETWEEN WEB DESIGNER AND WEBDEVELOPER

WEB DESIGNER

THEY DESIGN THE TEMPLATE IN PHOTOSHOP OR CORAL.

WEB DEVELOPER

THEY DEVELOP WEBSITES AND PROGRAMME THE WHOLE WEBSITE.

```
<HTML>

<head>

<link rel="stylesheet" type="text/css" href="didderences.css"/>

</head>
```

```html
<body>
<div class="heading">
<h3>difference between web designer and web developer</h3>
<div class="col 1">
<h3>web designer</h3>
<span>* THEY DESIGN THE TEMPLATE  IN PHOTOSHOP OR CORAL.
</span>
</div>
<div class="col 2">
<h3>web developer</h3>
<span>* THEY DEVELOP WEBSITES AND PROGRAMME  THE WHOLE WEBSITE.</span>
</div>
</div>
</body>
```

```
</html>

Code 2 for css

.heading

{position:relative;

Background-color:green;

Width:400px;

Text-align:center;

}

.col 1

{position:absolute;

Margin-top:50px;

Margin-left:0px;

Width:200px;

Background-color:purple;

}

{ position:absolute;

Margin-top:50px;
```

```
Margin-left:0px;

Width:200px;

}

Span

{display:block;

Text-align:left;

}
```

PROJECT

NOW before going to javascript lets make a project with css and html.

I don't want you to see the codes but you can see it if you have any problem and use photoshop to take images from it.

This is the html coding:-

```
<html>
<head>
<meta http-equiv="Content-Type" content="text/html; charset=utf-8" />
<title>Untitled Document</title>
<link href="mycss.css" rel="stylesheet" type="text/css" />
</head>

<body>
<div id="head">
<div class="txt1">
<font size="+3">Environmental.com</font><br />
```

```html
    <div align="right">site slogan
here</div></div>
    <div class="txt2">Helpline 24/7 Support
3246 345</div>
    <div class="feather"></div>


    <div class="heading">


    </div>
    <div class="middle">


    <div class="mid">
    <div class="text">
    <h1>Suspendius felis. Aenean<br />
     pulvinar vulpate nunc<br />Pellentesque
ultrics elit<br />vitaeo justo</h1></div>
    <div class="image"></div>
    </div>
```

```
<div class="image2"></div>

<div class="text4"><font
size="+1">Pellentesque vestibulum
erat.</font><br />Duis nisl. Cras a quam non
leo placerat lacinia. Proin in nulla. Sed a ligula
at quam vulputate auctor. Vivamus mi lacus,
feugiat eget, porta ut, fermentum nec, nisi.
Maecenas vel orci eu nunc accumsan
scelerisque. Class aptent taciti sociosqu ad
litora torquent per conubia nostra, per
inceptos himenaeos. Duis luctus sapien eu leo.
Etiam hendrerit leo eu metus. Morbi sagittis.
Nulla lacinia justo quis lorem. </div>


<div class="inbox"><div
class="greenhead"><font size="+2"><div
align="center">Maecenas
suscipit</div></font></div>

<div class="textinbox"><u>Nulla in velit nec
metus pharetra<br /><br />bibendum. Donec
metus leo, feugiat <br /><br />
```

sed, aliquet facilisis, pulvinar ac, mauris

vehicula venenatis arcu. Aenean

viverra consectetur neque. Aliquam

blandit bibendum lacus. In non nisi.

</u></div>

</div>

<div class="text5"><font size="+1">Nullam vitae leo vel pede sollicitudin suscipit</font>
<font size="-1">Nulla in velit nec metus pharetra bibendum. Donec metus leo, feugiat sed, aliquet facilisis, pulvinar ac, mauris. In feugiat sagittis nunc. Maecenas vehicula venenatis arcu. Aenean viverra consectetur neque. Aliquam blandit bibendum lacus. In non nisi. Fusce facilisis pulvinar tellus. Ut vitae purus ac odio fringilla

pulvinar. Quisque consectetur, urna sit amet fringilla tempus, neque nunc consequat eros, ac dignissim quam elit vel turpis. Donec sollicitudin mauris at purus suscipit sodales. Nunc rutrum ornare lacus. Maecenas accumsan turpis sit amet arcu</font></div>

<div class="text6"><font size="+1" color="#009933">Nullam vitae leo vel pede sollicitudin suscipit</font>
<font size="-1" color="#666666">Nulla in velit nec metus pharetra bibendum. Donec metus leo, feugiat sed, aliquet facilisis, pulvinar ac, mauris. In feugiat sagittis nunc. Maecenas vehicula venenatis arcu. Aenean viverra consectetur neque. Aliquam blandit bibendum lacus. In non nisi. Fusce facilisis pulvinar tellus. Ut vitae purus ac odio fringilla pulvinar. Quisque consectetur, urna sit amet fringilla tempus, neque nunc consequat eros, ac dignissim quam elit vel turpis. Donec sollicitudin mauris at purus suscipit sodales. Nunc rutrum ornare

lacus. Maecenas accumsan turpis sit amet arcu.</font></div>

<div class="button"><div align="center">

Read more</div>

<div class="text7"><font size="-3">Posted : 11-2-2009 11:45am by : Matthew Doyle</font></div>

</div>

</div>

<div class="foot"><div class="textfoot"><div align="center">Copyright © 2009 Environmental.com. All Rights Reserved</div></div>

</div>

</div>

</body>

</html>

This is css coding:-

```css
#head
{height:1024px;
width:1024px;
background-image:url(back.png);
background-color:#000;
}
.heading
{height:49px;
width:1024;
background-image:url(heading.png);
margin-top:114px;
}
.mid
```

```css
{height:293px;

width:1024px;

background-image:url(mid.png);

}

.middle

{height:822px;

width:1024px;

background-image:url(middle.png);

}

.foot

{height:50px;

width:1024px;

background-image:url(foot.png);

}

.text

{

    height:174px;
```

```
    width:489px;

    margin-top:40px;

    margin-left:56px;

}

.image

{

        height:226px;

        width:218px;

        float:right;

margin-right:20px;


background-image:url(plant.png);

}

.image2

{height:148px;

width:195px;

background-image:url(image.png);
```

```css
float:left;

margin-left:20px;

margin-top:20px;


}
.feather

{background-image:url(feather.png);

height:50px;

width:50px;

background-repeat:no-repeat;

margin-top:38px;

margin-left:43px;

}
.txt1

{height:54px;

width:304px;

float:left;
```

```css
margin-left:115px;

margin-top:38px;

color:#FFF;

}

.txt2

{height:16px;

width:235px;

color:#FFF;

float:left;

margin-top:51px;

margin-left:332px;

}

.inbox

{background-image:url(inbox.png);

height:295px;

width:273px;

float:right;
```

```css
    margin-right:28px;

    margin-top:60px;

}

.greenhead

{

    background-image:url(inboxhead.png);

    height:39px;

    width:271px;

    color:#FFF;

}


#nav {

    width: 1024px;

    height:48px;

    margin: 0px 0px 0px 20px;

    background-image:url(images/nav.gif);

    background-repeat:no-repeat;
```

```css
        display:inline;

        float:left;


}
#nav a {

        font-size:18px;

        font-style:italic;

        color:#FFF;

        font-family:Georgia, "Times New
Roman", Times, serif;

        margin: 12px 0px 10px 0px;

        padding: 0px 30px 0px 30px;

        float:left;


}
#nav a:hover {

        color:#862e06;

        text-decoration:none;
```

```css
}
.text4
{
    height:130px;
    width:470px;
    float:left;
    margin-left:20px;
    margin-top:35px;;
    color:#0C6
}
.text5
{height:104px;
width:651px;
margin-top:190px;
margin-left:10px;


}
```

```css
.text6
{height:105px;
width:651px;
margin-left:20px;
margin-top:40px;
}
.button
{background-image:url(box.png);
height:31px;
width:112px;
background-repeat:no-repeat;
margin-left:20px;
float:left;
}
.text7
{height:13px;
width:235px;
```

```css
margin-top:26px;

margin-left:20px;

float:left;

}

.textinbox

{height:240px;

width:260px;

color:#CCC;

margin-left:10px;

margin-top:10px;

}

.textfoot

{height:18px;

width:338px;

color:#FFF;

margin-left:329px;

}
```

INTRODUCTION TO JAVASCRIPT

JAVASCRIPT facilitates dynamic generation of content within webpages on an occurrence of an action performed by user. Javascript ca perform calculations and can do all type of calculation part. It is of two types:-

→*client side javascript*: executes on users workstation.

→*server side javascript:* executes on the web server.

```
<html>
<body>
<script>
document.write("<h1>This is a heading</h1>");
document.write("<p>This is a paragraph.</p>");
```

```
</script>

</body>

</html>
```

Output-This is a heading

This is a paragraph.

In this document.write is used when you want to print something on the webpage.

7.2 to get an alert box,

```
<html>

<body>

 <button type="button"
onclick="alert('Welcome!')">Click
Me!</button>

 </body>

 </html>
```

7.3 javascript can change the content of element

```
<html>
<body>

<p id="demo">
JavaScript can change the content of an
 HTML element.
</p>

<script>
function myFunction()
{
x=document.getElementById("demo");  // Find the element
x.innerHTML="Hello JavaScript!";   // Change the content
}
```

```
</script>

<button type="button"
onclick="myFunction()">Click Me!</button>

</body>

</html>
```

In this programme we have created a paragraph by using <p>tag then we have created a id "demo" in a paragraph, then we have created a function by the name myfunction() and you can give whatever you want then in a variable "x" we call the data of paragraph in the variable by document.getElementById("demo"); then we enter in the variable "x" change the data of it to "hello javascript" by using x.innerHTML="hello javascript";

Then at last we have created a button and called the function in it.

Before going to next practical let us see what are conditional statements, they are used to check conditions like

Let a=25; and b=30;

If(a<b)

{document.write("a is greater")

}

Else

{document.write("b is greater"}

So see this what if operator does, now lets see the example.

7.4 to change html images

<html>

```
<body>

<script>

function changeImage()

{

element=document.getElementById('myimage')

if (element.src.match("bulbon"))

  {

  element.src="pic_bulboff.gif";

  }

else

  {

  element.src="pic_bulbon.gif";

  }

}

</script>

<img id="myimage" onclick="changeImage()"
```

src="pic_bulboff.gif" width="100" height="180">

<p>Click the light bulb to turn on/off the light</p>

</body>

</html>

In this we have made a function in the script as change image, in that function we have get the image from the image id which is created at the last then we have checked that image with the image of on bulb and said that if the images are same than set the bulboff image and if it is not same then change the image to bulbon image. Then at the last in image id we have called the change image() function.

7.5 project

Now your project is to understand the project which I will give to you so best of luck in doing that:-

→to change the color of text

```html
<html>
<body>
<p id="demo">
JavaScript can change the style of an HTML element.
</p>
<script>
function myFunction()
{
x=document.getElementById("demo") // Find the element
x.style.color="#ff0000";        // Change the style
}
</script>
<button type="button" onclick="myFunction()">Click Me!</button>
</body>
```

</html>

→to display text

<html>

<body>

<h1>My Web Page</h1>

<p id="demo">A Paragraph.</p>

<div id="myDIV">A DIV.</div>

<script>

```
document.getElementById("demo").innerHTML="Hello Dolly";

document.getElementById("myDIV").innerHTML="How are you?";
```

</script>

</body>

</html>

→to change the text

<html>

<body>

```html
<h1>My Web Page</h1>

<p id="myPar">I am a paragraph.</p>

<div id="myDiv">I am a div.</div>

<p>

<button type="button"
onclick="myFunction()">Try it</button>

</p>

<script>

function myFunction()

{

document.getElementById("myPar").innerHTML="Hello Dolly";

document.getElementById("myDiv").innerHTML="How are you?";

}

</script>

<p>When you click on "Try it", the two elements will change.</p>
```

```
</body>
</html>
```

→to change properties of text

```html
<html>
<body>
<h1 id="myH1"></h1>
<p id="myP"></p>
<script>
// Write to a heading:
document.getElementById("myH1").innerHTML="Welcome to my Homepage";
// Write to a paragraph:
document.getElementById("myP").innerHTML="This is my first paragraph.";
</script>
<p><strong>Note:</strong> The comments
are not executed.</p>
</body>
```

</html>

7.6 CALCULATIONS IN JAVASCRIPT

NOW lets see how calculations are done in java

```html
<html>

<body>

<p id="myP"></p>

<script>

var x=5;

var y=x+2;

document.getElementById("myP").innerHTML
=y

</script>

 </body>

</html>
```

In this we have created a variable x, a variable is a kind of storage where you can store any kind of value, it can be a number or a string.

We have store a value"2" in x and in another variable y we increased the x by 2 then we

get into the id which is"myp" then by using document.getElementById("myP").innerHTM L=y

We sent the element "y" to the paragraph id and displayed it.

See a good example to understand the variable concept-:

```
<html>

<body>


<script>

var x=5;

var y=6;

var z=x+y;

document.write(x + "<br>");

document.write(y + "<br>");

document.write(z + "<br>");
```

```
</script>

</body>

</html>
```

Output-5

6

11

lOOPS

8.1 Intro to loops

loops are used when you want display same results again and again or same pattern of results like counting.

```
<script>

For(i=1; i≤10; i++)

{document.write(i);
```

```
}
</script>
```

This will display counting till 10.

→Like a table of 19

```
<script>
For(i=1; i≤10; i++)
{document.write(19*i);
}
</script>
```

8.2 WHILE LOOPS

Like for loop while loop also has same concept and same use like

```
<script>
While(i≤10)
{document.write(i)
i++}
</script>
```

8.3 breaks

We are going to learn how to break a loop

```html
<html>

<body>


<p>Click the button to do a loop with a break.</p>

<button onclick="myFunction()">Try it</button>

<p id="demo"></p>


<script>

function myFunction()

{

var x="",i=0;

for (i=0;i<10;i++)

  {

  if (i==3)
```

```
        {

        break;

        }

    x=x + "The number is " + i + "<br>";

    }

document.getElementByld("demo").innerHTM
L=x;

    }

    </script>

    </body>

    </html>
```

Output – the number is 0

 The number is 1

The number is 2

www.ingramcontent.com/pod-product-compliance
Lightning Source LLC
Chambersburg PA
CBHW041144050326
40689CB00001B/480